Mary Stuart, Bothwell, And The Casket Letters

John Watts De Peyster

In the interest of creating a more extensive selection of rare historical book reprints, we have chosen to reproduce this title even though it may possibly have occasional imperfections such as missing and blurred pages, missing text, poor pictures, markings, dark backgrounds and other reproduction issues beyond our control. Because this work is culturally important, we have made it available as a part of our commitment to protecting, preserving and promoting the world's literature. Thank you for your understanding.

KEEP COVER AND BIND IT AS TITLE PAGE AND INDEX.

MARY STUART, BOTHWELL,
AND THE
Casket Letters.
SOMETHING NEW.

WITH ILLUSTRATIONS AND PORTRAITS SELECTED FROM
HUNDREDS OF SPECIMENS FROM SCOTLAND,
ENGLAND, FRANCE, RUSSIA, &c.

"Go, draw aside the curtains, and discover
The several Caskets" * * *
"The first, of gold ["silver-overgilt"], who this inscription bears,—
Who chooseth me shall gain what many men desire."
—MERCHANT OF VENICE, II., 7.

"Fair glass of light, I lov'd you, and could still,
Were not the glorious CASKET *stored with ill:*——
—PERICLES, PRINCE OF TYRE, I., 1.

BOTHWELL'S BOOK STAMP.

"HARPAGON.—Et cette CASETTE [Chatoulle] comment est elle faite?"
"MAITRE JACQUES. * * * * *Elle est p tite,* si on le prendre par la ; mais *je l'appelle*
GRANDE POUR CE QU'ELLE CONTIENT."
—MOLIERE.

BY

 J. WATTS DE PEYSTER.

New York:
CHARLES H. LUDWIG, PRINTER, 10 & 12 READE STREET.
1890.

"Since this volume has been in the press, I have been enabled to add three portraits,—* * * The frontispiece [herewith presented] is reproduced, by the kind permission of his Grace, the Duke of Devonshire, and of the Marquis of Hartington, from the famous 'SHEFFIELD PORTRAIT,' preserved in Hardwick Hall. The original is printed on oak panel, and represents the Queen, in her thirty-sixth year, as anything but the beautiful woman traditionally described. *She has, also, a very decided cast in the right eye,* which the artist with some skill has rendered less obvious by representing her as looking towards the left. The upper portion of the picture, down to the hands, is reproduced in this volume with striking fidelity; but the lower part of the dress, the table on the right, and the carpet on which the Queen stands, though approximately correct, are not entirely so, owing to the difficulty of expressing in photography so dark an image as this old painting shows. The work has been skillfully executed by Messrs. Ad. Braum & Co., of Paris, from photographs prepared by Mr. J. Stringfellow, of Sheffield."

"MARY, *Queen of Scots,* IN CAPTIVITY: a narrative of events from January, 1569, to December, 1584, whilst George, Earl of Shrewsbury, was the guardian of the Scottish Queen." By John Daniel Leader. Sheffield: Leader & Sons; London: George Bell & Sons. 1880.

Holyrood Palace.

INTRODUCTION.

STRENUOUS efforts were made to exhibit in a Quartette of carefully elaborated works on Mary Stuart, Queen of Scots, the whole truth connected with her history while in Scotland, up to the date of her escape into England in 1568, particularly as regarded her relations with Bothwell. In the prosecution of these investigations, an unique and extensive library was collected in the course of ten years, which has been presented to Columbia College and there speaks for itself. Of all the authorities which it comprises, the last as to date of publication is in many respects the most important as to her culpability,—T. F. Henderson's "The Casket Letters and Mary Queen of Scots," from the press of Adam and Charles Black, Edinburgh, 1889, which is cited at length herewith, as conclusive evidence of the guilt of Mary. It establishes to the satisfaction of every non-partisan, unprejudiced and clear-headed student that Mary was guilty of the worst that has been charged against her; that she was an active and not a silent accomplice in the murder of her husband Darnley; that she loved, and loved best of all, the loyal James Hepburn, Earl of Bothwell, her third and last husband, and lured him by her "arts and part" to his ruin; and that instead of his being the "betrayer"—as he has always been represented by the champions of Mary—he was the "betrayed" both of her and of

Mary Queen of Scots.

almost the whole body of the Scottish nobility, who for, at that period, ruthless greed and crime could scarcely be equalled in any other country in Christendom, horrible and disgusting as were all the rest.

Any reader who takes an interest in the revelation of historical truth is referred to the writer's previous works: "Mary Queen of Scots, a Study," New York, 1882; "A Vindication of James Hepburn, fourth Earl of Bothwell, Philadelphia, 1882; "An Enquiry into the Career of Mary Stuart and a Justification of Bothwell," New York, 1883; and "Bothwell, an Historical Drama," New York, 1884.

Mary Queen of Scots.

While in the collection of hundreds of authorities above referred to, no two seem to agree, altogether, when the result is carefully strained, sifted or dissected out. The writer has likewise collected almost as many hundreds of portraits of Mary, no two of which agree. Not more than three have any claims to authenticity, and their differences cannot be reconciled if there is any foundation, even, to their claims as likenesses. It is asserted and it is extremely likely that the statement is founded on facts

Mary Queen of Scots.

pretty well established, that the most attractive picture which we have of Mary Stuart is not hers at all, but a portrait of Ida, or Agnes, Countess of Mansfelt, who, driven by persecution from

Germany, took refuge in England and was thence expelled by that jealous vanity of Elizabeth, who neither would nor could tolerate female loveliness in a court or circle in which the basest adulation accepted her ugliness as the highest type of womanly beauty and to the disgrace of truth and manhood glorified it as such.

Mary Queen of Scots was in very truth anything but that which she is almost universally accepted as having been. She was not either delicate of form and feature and of the average size of her sex. She was not fascinatingly beautiful, while perfectly fascinating in her alluring ways and infinite deceptiveness. She was rather of a rough texture than a refined, but possessed

Darnley.

of that most extraordinary of gifts, the art of concealing art, in addition to the graces conferred by education and environment; and, being a crowned head, she was accepted as a combined goddess of love and regal majesty, which certainly could not have been the case had she occupied a lower rank. Her mother,

Mary of Lorraine, is handed down by tradition, supported by historical research, as the tallest and largest woman in Europe; and if Mary did not equal her in development of frame and height, she was an exceedingly tall, long-limbed and muscular woman, so tall that she over-topped her second husband, Darnley, who was recognized for his excessive attitude as the "long laddie," standing over six feet. Mary was robust in texture, capable of supporting fatigue and privation, and competent to thrive on

Bothwell.

rough fare, hard treatment and strenuous exertion sufficient to tax the fibres of athletic men, innured by life-long practice to exercises which would test the most hardy and healthy male specimens, accustomed to outdoor pursuits, at the present day.

On the other hand, Bothwell has been reviled as old and ugly. He was neither, but the contrary. He was not born earlier than 1535, and when he first encountered Mary in France—in 1560 after the death of her first husband, Francis II.—she was born in 1542—and fell in love with her, he was between twenty-five and twenty-seven and she was eighteen, just about the proper disparity in years for a union between the sexes. He was tall, athletic, finely formed, a brave soldier, an able leader, an accomplished knight, a noble of ancient lineage, of high rank and standing, endowed with many gifts of mind, a lover of books and setting high value upon them, fond of rich bindings with an exquisite Book-mark, loyal to the core; and for his time, place and country, well educated. Besides his native Scotch, he spoke to some degree polished English, and understood, spoke and wrote French. He also knew Latin and, far more than his colleagues, what are understood as the "Humanities." As a man he was by no means below Mary as a woman, and as for his peers in Scotland, he was, as he has been styled by an acute foreign writer, a German, by nature most critical, that *rara avis*, a white crow amid a flock of black ones—a white crow in every sense, white in the inner as in the outer man. Moreover despite his fidelity to the Regent Mary, and to Mary Stuart herself, he was a Protestant to the core and he made Mary tolerant.

Unfortunate Bothwell. Far ahead of his time in his desire to organize an equitable rule for Scotland; honest in his views and intentions, if honesty and politics are reconcilable.

This monograph, however, is not intended as an additional vindication of Bothwell, because it would be impossible to present further proofs for his perfect exoneration than have already been aggregated in the Tetralogy—four preceding works—of which this completes the Pentapla.

The same is not the fact in regard to Mary, because new testimony has been discovered since the preceding Tetralogy was issued from the press. This new testimony places beyond doubt the genuineness of the Casket Letters and Documents, and Mary cannot escape the judgment of guilty. Perhaps her innocence would never have been championed if she had not been constituted the banner bearer of Roman Catholicism and elevated into a martyr for Papalism. She has been justly styled "the forlorn hope of the old Catholic Faith in Scotland," and it has been the "theory of the ecclesiastics" that, as far as regarded any participation, covert or overt, in the murder of her second husband, Darnley, she was "innocent as a child, immaculate as a saint." Some of her defenders, however, have assumed for her a middle position between positive complicity and absolute innocence, but her exceptional courage, fertility of resource, strength of will and other marked characteristics preclude the possibility of anything like indifference or neutrality. Her attitude towards the man charged with being the chief conspirator against Darnley— some writers claim his real name was Darley—Bothwell, was not of a merely passive kind. She could not have been blind to the fact that Bothwell was in love with her. All the evidence, apart even from the Casket Letters, coincide that she was in love with him. Presenting the best case for her that is possible, if she married him at last unwillingly, she knew the reward that he claimed and she granted the reward to which for years he had aspired.

> "Lucretia Borgia, thou, in facile change
> Of husbands, lovers, favorites, and friends;
> And Serpent of the Nile in charming ways
> That never staled nor satisfied desire;
> And yet without all pity as the first,
> Chameleon, like the other, in thy moods;
> Cruel as both, oblivious of the man
> Whom first you sought and caught, so soon betray'd."

"The fatal weakness, indeed, if all such arguments as are used to establish either Mary's absolute or partial innocence of the murder, is that they do not harmonize with the leading traits of her disposition. She was possessed of altogether exceptional

DEATH of RIZZIO.

decision and force of will; she was remarkably wary and acute; and she was a match for almost any of her contemporaries in the art of diplomacy. She was not one to be concussed into a course of action to which she had any strong aversion, and in all matters vitally affecting herself was in the habit of using her own independent judgment.

"*Her conduct during the three months succeeding the murder* [of Darnley] *can, however, only be regarded as consistent with her innocence on the supposition*, to use the cogent words of Mr. Swinburne, that '*this conduct was a tissue of such dastardly imbecility, such heartless irresolution, and such brainless inconsistency, as forever to dispose of her time-honored claim to the credit of intelligence and courage.*'"

The trial of Bothwell for the murder of Darnley was notoriously and palpably delusive, and his acquittal a foregone conclusion for the responsibility of which no casuistry can absolve Mary. For any one but a partisan to manufacture excuses for an out and out Roman Catholic consenting to a marriage with a man divorced by her connivance, for the occasion, is an utter perversion of common sense, of truth and of honesty. That she consented to a separation from Bothwell at Carberry Hill would be unaccountable in any woman except one belonging to that rare class to which Mary must be assigned, and her changeful moods between the night of Kirk-o'-Field and Carberry Hill—as at previous dates while Darnley was yet alive—are at least as consistent with guilt as with innocence. Few readers or students of her case seem to be aware that she had a child or twins by Bothwell in Loch Levin Castle, and scarcely any dwell upon likelihood that the very resignation that she was forced to subscribe was obtained from her by the threat, while she was suffering from the severe effects of premature child-bearing, of publishing the contents of the Casket Letters, &c.

Hosack, her excuser, allowed himself to be deluded by a mere title, which did not set forth and inadequately represented Morton's "Declaration," which settled beyond doubt why, when, and how the Casket Letters and other criminating documents were obtained. That declaration, as it was written and was attested, did not reach the eyes of the public until within a year, and even then, thus late, only through the research of Mr. Henderson. He shows with legal ability that the letters were genuine. Whether the letters were written in Scotch or in French matters but little. If in the former, the whole bulk of the evidence goes to show that they were not written to Darnley, as some of her defenders and extenuators claim. If written in French, Darnley did not understand that language and Bothwell assuredly did. That the original letters have disappeared is of little importance. The testimony of Cecil, so awfully distorted, was nevertheless absolutely clear. It substantiates that the Casket Letters, &c., "were duly conferred and compared" before the English Commissioners. It is also shown by cumulative proofs that the originals so exhibited must have been made way with by those into whose power they eventually fell and who were immediately interested in their disappearance.

To allege that the style and contents of the letters were unworthy of a refined woman, has no weight, because a woman in love with a man with whom she has no right so to be and is fired with passion, as a rule, almost without exception, is characterized by such wanton oblivion of propriety of expression and language as are manifested throughout in the Casket Letters. The animal instincts then over-ride, spur, lash and direct the pen, and it would be just as sensible to submit the question of such compositions to a jury of cold, chaste, religious women as to another of younger members of the same sex, upon whose innocence no stain of the knowledge of good and evil as yet had fallen, or such *ingenus* as are totally ignorant of the ways and wantonness of this "wicked, wicked world." Another weak argument against the alleged genuineness of the Casket Letters is some discrepancy in dates. When those who are observant of such matters come to reflect, they will at once arrive at the conclusion that there is nothing more common than the confounding of dates when the mind is not strongly directed to the necessity of accuracy. Such mistakes occur daily. How much more likely were they to occur when diaries were uncommon and not lying about on every table, conspicuously clear in print.

These arguments seem all that is necessary to introduce a citation of the two most important chapters of Mr. Henderson's convincing work—convincing to any one who has not made up his mind not to allow himself to be affected by any testimony. With a Roman Catholic it is useless to argue in regard to one of his "forlorn hopes" or martyrs, especially because the system he recognizes as unassailable is founded on fiction—beginning with the assertion that Peter was the first Pope of Rome for twenty-five years, when it cannot be proved that he ever was in that city;—on fabrications—simply citing one as one example, the false Decretals;—on fallacies—manifested by the perversion of texts and every kind of testimony bearing on the legitimacy of the Papacy or its dogmas. Nor is it worth while to waste a word on lukewarm Protestants, who seem not to dare to defend their own cause, and deserve the severe adjuration addressed to the Church of Laodicea, "because thou art lukewarm, and neither cold nor hot, I will spew thee out of my mouth." Erastians—the term once expressive of such bitter feeling in Scotland—are equally inaccessible to reason and to proof. Finally, there is a class who are so high in the clouds of transcendental admiration of Mary that it is impossible to bring them down into an atmosphere of common sense.

Finally, to recapitulate in "summing up," Mary, so far from being a victim to the audacious wiles of Bothwell, the latter was the victim of the fascinations of the Queen; and the "Casket Letters," Sonnets, &c., were authentic and have been conclusively shown so to be. One argument advanced by the defenders of the Queen were the circumstances under which those "Casket Letters and Sonnets" fell into the hands of the Rebel Lords, who afterwards made such good use of them to prove her guilt, which had been previously palpable to every one in Scotland who was not carried away and blinded to the truth by Romanist bigotry, Jacobite delusion or invincible obstinacy. It was always claimed that Morton did not obtain the Casket with the Letters and Sonnets in the way and manner that impartiality presented the matter, but that the narrative and the capture, as well as the alleged contents of the Casket, were both forgeries and falsifications. The Marian party were either ignorant that Morton made a Declaration which cleared up, or away, every difficulty, or, if cognizant of the fact, perverted its language or denied its validity or even it existence.—T. F. Henderson, in the "Casket 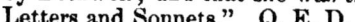 Letters and Mary Queen of Scots," published at Edinburgh by Charles and Adam Black, 1889, chapter VII., page 90, &c., has made everything clear and incontrovertible.

Who ever will read what follows, and particularly the Declaration, marked A, among the Appendices, and will *still* DENY that Morton and his associates did fairly get possession of the Casket containing the Letters and Sonnets, &c., of Mary, and that the latter were written by her, as they appear, and by no other, would not be convinced of her guilt, even though she arose from the dead and made full confession of having had "art and part" in the murder of Darnley; that she was the whole cause of the assiduous and assured course of procedure pursued by Bothwell; and that she was the sole author of the "Casket Letters and Sonnets." Q. E. D.

THE EARL OF MORTON'S DECLARATION.

(From Folio 216 of No. 32,091 of the Additional MSS. in the British Museum.)

(Appendix A. Pages 113-116, "The Casket Letters and Mary Queen of Scots, with Appendices." By T. F. Henderson. Edinburgh: Adam and Charles Black, 1889.)

THE true Declaration and Report [Anglicized] of me, JAMES, EARL OF MORTON, how a certain *Silver Box, over gilt,* containing divers missive writings, sonnets, contracts and obligations for marriage between the Queen-mother [*i.e.,* MARY], mother to our sovereign Lord [James VI.], and JAMES, sometime EARL OF BOTHWELL, was found and used.

Morton.

Upon Thursday, the 19th of June, 1567, I dined at Edinburgh; the L. of Ledington, Secretary, with me. At time of my dinner a certain man came to me, and in secret manner showed me that three servants of the Earl of Bothwell (viz.: Mr. Thomas Hepburn, parson of Auldhamesokkes, John Coc(k)burn, brother to the Lord of Stirling, and George Dalgleische) were coming to the town, and passed into the castle. Upon which advice I on the sudden [suddenly] sent my cousin, Mr. And. Douglas and Robert Douglas his brother, and James Johnstoun of Westerrall, with others my servants to the number of sixteen or thereabouts, toward the Castle and make search for the said persons and, if possible, there to apprehend them. According to which, my directions, my servants past [went]; and at the first missing the first-named three persons, because they were departed forth from the Castle before their coming, my men then parting in several companies upon knowledge that the others whom they sought were separated. Mr. And. Douglas sought for Mr. Thomas Hepburn and found him not, but got his horse; James Johnstoun sought for Jo Coc(k)burn and apprehended him; Robert Douglas seeking for George Dalgleische, after he had almost given up his search and inquisition, a good fellow, understanding his purpose, came to him and offered for a mean piece of money to reveal where George Dalgleische was. The same [Robert Douglas] satisfying him that gave the intelligence for his pains, passed to the Potteraw [Potter-row, College Street], before Edinburgh, and there apprehended the said George, with divers evidences and letters in parchment, viz.: the Earl Bothwell's investments of Liddisdale, of the Lordship of Dunbar and of Orkney, and divers co^{r}is [copies?] which all with the said George [Dalgleische] himself, the said Robert [Douglas] brought and presented to me. And the said George, being examined of the cause of his direction to the Castle of Edinburgh and what letters and evidences he brought forth of the same, alleged he was sent to inspect Lord Bothwell, his master's clothing, and that he had not any letters nor commodities, nor [neither] they which were apprehended with him; but his report being found suspicious and his gesture and behaviour ministering [exhibiting] cause of mistrust, seeing the gravity of the action that was in hand, it was resolved by common consent of the noblemen convened that the said George Dalgleische should be surely kept that night and upon the morn should be taken to the Tolbooth of Edinburgh and there put in the pain [torture] and tormented for furthering the declaration of the truth, which [the torture] being set upon [for] Friday, the 20th day of the same month of June, before any rigorous demeaning of his person, seeing the pain [torture to be endured] and moving of conscience, he called for my cousin, Mr. And. Douglas, who coming, the said George desired that Robert Douglas should be sent with him, and he would show and bring to light that which he had. Then, being taken forth from the pain [*peine fort et dure*, Fr. for torture] he passed with the said Robert to the Potteraw [Potter-row, College Street], and there, under the seat of a bed, took forth the said silver box, which he had brought forth from the Castle the day before, locked, and brought the same to me at 8 hours at night. And, because it was late, I kept it all that night. Upon the [next] morning, viz., Saturday, the 21st June, in presence of the Earls of Athol, Mar, Glencairn and myself, The Lords Home, Sempill, Sanquhar, the Master of Grahame, and the Secretary [Lethington] and Laird of Tullibarden, Comptroller, and the said And. Douglas, the said box was stricken up [broken open] because we wanted the key [the key was not forthcoming], and the letters it contained were sichtet [*i.e.*, carefully inspected] and immediately thereafter delivered again into my hand and custody. Since which time I have observed and kept the same box and all letters, missives, contracts, sonnets and various writings contained therein, surely, without alteration, changing, increasing or diminishing of anything found or received in the said box.

This I testify and declare to be undoubted truth.

This is the copy of that which was given to Mr. Secretary Cecil upon Thursday, the 8th of December, 1568.

This is the true copy of the declaration made and presented by the Earl of Morton to the Commissioners and Council of England, sitting in Westminster for [at] the time, upon Thursday, being the 29th of December, 1568.

Subscribed with his hand thus,

[Signed,] MORTON.

Ruins of Dunbar Castle.

Edinburgh Castle.

HENDERSON.—Chapter VII.—VIII., page 90 to 110. "The Casket Letters and Mary Queen of Scots." By T. F. Henderson. Edinburgh: Adam and Charles Black. 1889.

[Caps, Italics, Fists, &c., inserted for emphasis and to attract attention by J. W. de P.]

"MORTON'S DECLARATION, like the CASKET DOCUMENTS, has been lost, and until the publication of the *Fifth Report of the Historical Manuscript Commission* no copy of it was known to exist. ☞The Commissioners gave what appeared to be a *succinct* SUMMARY of the document, but it is a summary resembling a description of the play of Hamlet without any reference to Hamlet himself. ☞ In 1883, the manuscripts of Sir Alexander Malet were acquired by the Trustees of the British Museum, and the copy of the DECLARATION OF MORTON—which had been summarized by the Historical Commissioners—now forms folio 216 of No. 32,091 of the Additional MSS. Being desirous to know whether Morton merely declared in vague and general terms, that he had opened the CASKET in presence of "others," as the Historical MSS. Commissioners' Report has it, or whether the names of those present were given, I carefully examined the manuscript, and found it to contain *statements* of such vital consequence as *practically to be decisive in regard to the* AUTHENTICITY *of the documents*. [The Declaration is printed in full in Appendix A. See pages 13–15 hereof.] Its graphic and detailed picture of what, if it really did happen, was a very striking historical incident, bears, at least, all the external marks of truth. The copy is a contemporary one, and of its genuineness there can be no doubt whatever. The two cardinal points in the Declaration are: (1) that the Documents immediately after the Casket was opened, were "*sichted*;" and (2) the list of the noblemen and others by whom, Morton affirmed, they were "sichted."

The Scots verb to "sicht" is somewhat analogous to the German "*sichten*," and is defined by Jamieson as "*to view narrowly, to inspect*." Jamieson illustrates its meaning by the two following examples: "The Moderator craved that these books might be *sighted* by Argyle, Lauderdale, and Southesk." (Baillie's Letters, I., 113); "At this assembly Dr. Sibbald, late Minister of Aberdeen, his papers which were taken from him were revised and *sighted*; some whereof smacked of Arminianism as they thought, and whilk they kept" (Spalding, I., 135.) The word was a technical, almost a legal term, applied specially to the inspection of documents. If the Documents in the Casket underwent such a process of inspection on the 21st of June, 1567, it was practically impossible that they could have been afterwards exchanged for forged documents without the fraud being detected. In such an extraordinary crisis of affairs it was of the utmost importance for the Confederate Lords to know the precise tenor of the documents thus stated to have been discovered. Supposing the examination to have been *bona fide*, the casket would be opened with the utmost curiosity, and the documents read and considered with the greatest care. Even if there be the possibility that some of the documents were afterwards manipulated and altered, it is impossible to suppose that such an extraordinary document as Letter 2, *containing the main portion of the incriminating evidence* against the Queen, could have been fabricated subsequently, or that the two Contracts of Marriage could have been subsequently placed in the Casket.

What proof, then, did Morton adduce that they were "sichted"? [Answer!] A list of witnesses very formidable in numbers, and in regard to individuals as formidable almost as it could possibly have been. The names, in addition to that of Morton, are:— the Earls of Athol, Mar, and Glencairn, Lords Home, Semple, and Sanquhar, the Master of Graham, the Secretary (Maitland of Lethington), the Laird of Tullibardine and Mr. Andrew Douglas. ☞ *One peculiarity about the names*, worthy of special notice, *is that not one of them, with the exception of Morton, is affixed to the Bond*—as printed in Calderwood's "History of the Church of Scotland"—in favor of BOTHWELL, signed in *Ainslie's Tavern*. It would have been egregious folly in Morton to have inserted in the list of those present at the "sichting" of the documents the names of any who were *not* present, or who were *not* prepared to assert that they were present. Such a fraud would inevitably, sooner or later, have been detected. In any case, the Regent [Murray] and Morton, however daring they might be, were too sagacious to run such a tremendous risk. They were by no means certain of their position with Elizabeth —indeed, certainty on such a point was an absolute impossibility. On the supposition that MARY did not write the letters, they were, by giving in a false list of witnesses, supplying the most certain means of detection. Moreover, among the English noblemen before whom the whole of the papers were laid were those who, in the words of Mr. Froude, "had made themselves most conspicuous as the advocates of the Queen of Scots," including the [Roman] *Catholic* Earls of Norfolk, Westmoreland, and Northumberland. But before these Catholic nobles of England, Morton ventured to adduce Athol, the leader of the Catholics of Scotland, and several other Catholic noblemen, *as witnesses for the genuineness* of the documents. Nor did he know, when he gave in his Declaration on the 9th of December, what exact turn the discussion might take; the English Commissioners, or any one of them, might have declined to accept the Declaration unless confirmed by special inquiry of the persons mentioned; it was even then by no means impossible that Mary—especially if she did not write the letters—would agree to some form of enquiry which would lead to the whole evidence being placed before her. On any supposition, therefore, it is impossible to believe that Morton adduced as witnesses persons who were not present, or were not prepared to swear that they were present. But Athol's testimony is almost of itself conclusive of the inspection of the documents. He had left the party of the Queen from entirely disinterested motives, and, being a Catholic, it is impossible to conceive that he would knowingly conspire to blast the reputation of a Catholic sovereign. Besides, he again became the leader of the Catholics in their policy against the Regency, and ultimately was one of Morton's most bitter enemies; but there is no evidence that he ever on any occasion expressed doubts regarding the genuineness of the CASKET DOCUMENTS, although the exposure of the forgery would have rendered an almost inestimable service to the cause of the Queen. Among other witnesses who subsequently supported the Queen was Lord HOME, who joined KIRKALDY OF GRANGE in the romantic defense of the Castle of Edinburgh, and who is described by Sir James Melville as "so true a Scotsman that he was unwinnable to do anything prejudicial to his country." The Deposition of Lord Home (Note A) in regard to the Regent Moray is entirely consistent with Sir James Melville's estimate, and both it and the Deposition of Kirkaldy of Grange must be held to refute the surmise of Mr. Skelton that Kirkaldy of Grange (Note B), Lord Home, or any other leading supporter of Moray, left Moray because in producing the *Casket Letters* he had "lent himself to a fraud." The other names include two Catholics,—Semple and the Laird of Tullibardine; Sanquhar, who, with Tullibardine, signed the bond for Mary's deliverance from Lochleven; and the Master of Graham, who, as the third Earl of Montrose, conspired with Argyle and Atholl to bring about Morton's fall in 1578, and afterwards had a prominent share in bringing him to the scaffold. In addition to these names, special importance attaches to the name of the Earl of Mar, whom Sir James Melville specially characterizes as a "trew nobleman," and who, by his moderation and fairness of spirit, had won the high respect of both parties. ☞ The testimony of these noblemen must be accepted as decisive at least regarding the fact of the "*sichting*" of the documents. If the documents were forged, the forgery must have been completed before that date. Lord Herries, the advocate of Queen Mary, while admitting the discovery of the Casket, asserted that Morton had exchanged genuine documents for false ones. If he did so, this must have happened on the night of the 20th. ☞ There is, of course, the initial difficulty that Morton did not have the key, which was presumedly in the possession of Bothwell; but, in any case, the exchange could not have been effected in the presence of the noblemen above mentioned.

The character and position of perhaps the most notable witness to the "*sichting*" of the documents, namely Maitland of Lethington, remains yet to be considered. Maitland was present both at the York and Westminster Conferences, but even by his colleagues he was distrusted: "all Scotland knew," in the words of Mr. Skelton, "that Maitland was on Mary's side;" he had been nicknamed by the Regent and his friends "the necessary evil;" the Regent, it was well known, had brought him with him to England, because he did not deem it safe to leave him at home; and, as a matter of fact, the Queen of Scots had, through his wife, Mary Fleming,—one of the "Queen's Maries,"—☞ been secretly supplied with a copy of one of the *versions* of the Letters. ☞ Notwithstanding Maitland's ambiguous attitude, Morton did not hesitate to declare on his solemn oath, *in Maitland's presence*, that the message regarding the mission of Bothwell's servants to the castle was sent to him while he was dining with Maitland in Edinburgh; that he gave orders for their apprehension in Maitland's presence; that the putting of George Dalgleish to the torture was resolved on "by common consent of the noblemen convened," including, of course, Maitland; and that Maitland was present when the Casket was opened on the 21st. ☞ *By this Declaration*, made in Maitland's presence, the word of Maitland was pledged, with an implication almost as absolute as that of Morton, for the genuineness of the documents. Referring to Maitland's attitude towards the accusations against Mary at the Conference, Mr. Skelton ☞ arrogates the right to assert that he "held himself aloof from the farce that was being played." ☞ Maitland's aloofness could not have been more than moral or intellectual, for bodily he was present, though possibly against his will. In view of Morton's declaration, the hypothesis even of mental or moral aloofness can scarcely, however, be regarded any longer as specially appropriate. ☞ Whether he wished it or not, the Declaration of Morton compelled Maitland to play a very prominent part in the farce, if it is to be reckoned a farce. ☞ Maitland must also be held chiefly responsible for the fact that the farce, if it was a farce, ended in such a mournful tragedy. Some fatal spell prevented him from *uttering a syllable of protest or explanation* when Morton made the explicit and detailed declaration virtually to the effect that Maitland knew as much about the documents as he did. ☞ It can hardly be maintained, on the supposition that the letters were a forgery, that this most skilled diplomatist, and, according to Mr. Skelton, the ablest man, at that time, in Scotland, if not even in Europe, was not completely outwitted; or, *that he was not made to act a part so sorry and contemptible* as to cause Mr. Skelton's eulogies on his character and abilities to sound like subtle irony. Had he only on this all momentous occasion exhibited *a faint gleam of that "scorn of pharisaic pretense,"* which, according to Mr. Skelton, "scorched like fire," ☞ how withering would have been the effect on Morton and his accomplices? The theory of Mr. Skelton seems to be that Maitland was "not a party to the deceit," and was ignorant of its innermost secret. ☞ On this theory Maitland might have allowed Morton to tell his own tale, *provided he refrained from falsehood as to Maitland's connection with the discovery* of the Casket; but to allow Morton to associate him so circumstantially with the opening of the casket was, *if Morton foreswore himself, to witness without an apparent symptom of regret the extinguishment of the last flicker of his* OWN *honor*. Diplomacy, it is true, has its own peculiar canons, but no canon, however "exceeding broad," can either excuse or explain such callous torpidity. But even were we to regard as possible the theory that Maitland in such extraordinary circumstances "would not have acted otherwise than he did," it is impossible to suppose that the Regent [Murray] and Morton had made such a theory the basis of their action, and that, if there was a damning secret, they were trusting to Maitland's eternal retention of it, except possibly on one of two suppositions: either that Maitland was concerned in the forgery, or was afraid of the consequences of his implication in Darnley's murder.

That Maitland was THE forger has been a favorite theory with those who deny the genuineness of the documents. This theory was even at one time held by Mr. Skelton: "The master wit of Lethington," he said, "was there to shape the plot; Lethington, with numberless scraps of the Queen's handwriting in his possession, and with a divine or diabolic spark of genius in his nature which might have made him on a large scale one of the leaders of mankind" (Note C). Although Mr. Skelton has not penned any recantation of this opinion, republished in 1876, it must be presumed that later information has led him to regard it as no longer tenable; for in the second volume of "*Maitland of Lethington*," published in 1888, the above theory is silently suppressed in favor of the Morton theory—"dissolute lawyers and unfrocked priests" being summoned by Mr. Skelton's imagination to execute the task for which the services of Maitland's "divine or diabolic" genius are no longer available. "Morton," he remarks, "one of the mercenaries of the Reformation, who, like others of his trade, combined craft with ferocity, had plenty of clever scamps in his pay—dissolute lawyers, unfrocked priests,—who, out of the mass of Mary's manuscripts which were found at Holyrood, could have manufactured with facility a score of letters to a lover" (Note D). Whether the Morton theory, as stated by Mr. Skelton, *with its whole bundle of assumptions*, be regarded as more credible or not than the Maitland theory, the latter theory has not only been abandoned but entirely refuted by Mr. Skelton. If in his volumes on Maitland of Lethington he has demonstrated anything, he has demonstrated that Maitland was incapable of committing such a forgery, or being an active party to such a conspiracy against the Queen of Scots. One of the main purposes of his volumes is to illustrate the fact that Maitland had always the best interests of the Queen at heart; and it would be straining our credulity too far to ask us to believe that Maitland had recourse to the forgery of the Casket Documents to promote the Queen's best interests. Opinions may differ as to whether Mr. Skelton has not formed too high an opinion of Maitland both morally and intellectually, both as a churchman and a statesman, but it can scarcely be doubted that he has been successful in removing from Maitland's reputation much undeserved obloquy, and in demonstrating that he was at least as consistent and unselfish in his conduct as the majority of politicians. Such a view of Maitland's character cannot be maintained if he had any connection with the forgery of the letters; and, even if it could, the fact that the forgery must have been completed before the 20th June, renders it impossible that he could have had any part in it. He had left the Queen as late as the 9th, and Morton was too prudent to have accepted the services of such a recruit in such a compromising enterprise. Indeed, there can scarcely be any doubt that Maitland only stated the truth in regard to his attitude to Mary at this time, when in a letter to Cecil of the 21st June (written probably immediately after the discovery of the Casket Documents), he said: "The reverence and affection I have ever borne to the Queen, my mistress, hath been the occasion to stay me so long in company with the Earl of Bothwell at the Court,—as my life hath every day been in danger since he began to aspire to any grandeur." ☞ It being thus impossible to conceive that Maitland was directly concerned in the concoction of the forgery, it remains to be considered whether his silent assent to Morton's declaration is explicable on the supposition of his implication in the murder of Darnley. In regard to Maitland's connection with the murder, Mr. Skelton has arrived at a verdict of "*not proven.*" This is certainly to take the most favorable view possible of Maitland's conduct, and, in arriving at it, Mr. Skelton has omitted any reference to the testimony of Bothwell's subordinate agents in regard to the Craigmillar Bond. For verdicts of "not proven" —a peculiarity of Scot's law—Mr. Skelton has a peculiar *penchant*, EXCEPT *where the opponents of Mary are concerned.* In regard to the heinous guilt of Moray, Morton, Knox, Cecil, and Elizabeth, he is untroubled by the smallest scruples of doubt; but the evidence must be very unimpeachable indeed that will compel him to admit any definite wrong-doing either in the case of Mary or of Maitland. That Maitland was directly involved in the plot against Darnley is at least more probable than that Moray or any of his more intimate colleagues were involved in it. He differed from them, however, in that he never disguised his dislike to Mary's marriage with Bothwell, and, as we have seen, in THAT he was sincerely devoted to the Queen's interests. ☞ If, therefore, he concealed the secret of the forgery, or allowed Morton falsely to declare that he was present at the opening of the Casket on the 21st June, *his conduct was simply that of a mean and craven dastard,—a dastard, moreover, so paralyzed by selfish fear, that his marvelous penetration and shrewdness altogether deserted him.* The theory that the Letters were a forgery can therefore be maintained by

Mr. Skelton, only *on condition that he revokes every favorable estimate he has formed of Maitland;* and, *vice versa,* the acceptance of the genuineness of the letters seems to be the chief thing wanting to establish Mr. Skelton's theory of Maitland's high-minded consistency. Deny the genuineness of the Letters, and Maitland's conduct *becomes inexplicable on any theory that allows him even a shred of honesty or ability;* but admit their genuineness, and most of the weak and inconsistent touches are removed from the striking historical portrait which, in many other respects, Mr. Skelton has limned with careful and felicitous skill. ☞ One conclusion, therefore, established beyond all doubt by the tenor of Morton's declaration, is that the Documents in the Casket were "*sichted*" on the 21st June. This at once disposes of the very strong objection that has been taken to Moray's receipt, the 16th September, 1568, testifying in the name of the Privy Council that Morton had "truly and honestly kept the said box," &c.

"But here," says Goodall, "it comes naturally to be questioned how Murray, or his Council, and especially he himself, who was in France at the time, could so readily and roundly attest, either that this Box and Letters were found with Dalgleish, or that Morton had so honestly preserved them all that time, without any manner of change or alteration? This seems repugnant to common-sense, and is so far from answering their purpose, that it affords the most vehement presumption of fraud" (Note E). This opinion has been echoed and emphasized by many subsequent writers, and by none with more impressive and pungent reiteration than by Mr. Skelton. "They remained," he caustically observes, "for another year in the custody of the precise and scrupulous Morton" (II., 279). "What was taken from the Casket, what was placed in the Casket, by Morton," he declares, "only Morton could tell; and Morton could keep his own counsel better than most men" (II., 308). "Seeing that the Casket," he further argues, "had been in Morton's custody for nearly fifteen months, it is hard to understand how Moray, untouched by any sense of shame, could have emitted such a declaration" (II., 313). He even represents the case as an illustration of the maxim, "He who excuses, accuses himself," for, says he, "Moray's assurance that the Box had not been tampered with since it was recovered, is calculated—for how could Moray know?—to intensify the suspicions it was meant to allay" (Ib., II., 313).

☞ Whatever force there may have been in such aphorisms previous to the discovery of Morton's Declaration, it is indisputable that that Declaration robs them of all their significance and sting. Not only so, but if the Thesis of Forgery is to be maintained, the whole chain of argument against the genuineness of the Documents must be constructed anew from the very beginning. If the forgery was completed by the 20th June,—or only six days after Mary's surrender at Carberry Hill,—not only was it *impossible* for Crawford's declaration to be supplied to the forgers, but we must premise an almost *superhuman promptness*, both of purpose and execution, to admit the possibility of manufacturing them out of the "mass of Mary's manuscripts found at Holyrood"—even supposing such a "mass" had been found—within such a limited time. To maintain the hypothesis of forgery, we are thus compelled to remove the date of the occurrence back to a period even anterior to Mary's capture at Carberry. The idea of a forgery, completed at such an early date, can scarcely be seriously entertained by even the most prejudiced defender of the Queen; and its probability does not, therefore, require any discussion."

James Stuart (Murray).

Ruins of Bothwell Castle.

"CONCLUSION (Chapter VIII.)—One of the circumstances that has been regarded as most strongly corroborative of the genuineness of the Casket Documents is the almost *unbroken silence* in reference to them maintained by MARY and her friends. When the silence was broken by Mary, it was under the compulsion of stern necessity, and the language made use of was *indecisive* and *ambiguous*. All that she instructed her Commissioners to say was: "I never writ anything concerning that matter to any creature; and gif ony sic writings, be they are false and feinzeiet forgit and invent be thamselfis, onlye to my dishonour and sclander; and thair ar divers in Scotland baith men and women, that can counterfeit my handwriting, and write the like maner of writing quhilk I use, as weill as myself, and principallie sic as ar in companie with thameselfis."

This *denial*, such as it is, is *deprived of all validity* by the fact that Mary denied much more emphatically her authorship of the letters to Babington, the genuineness of which has now been conclusively established. The denial is, however, a mere formal device, which probably did not deceive even her Commissioners, and amounts to little more than a *transparent quibble*. Her defenders denied, and she would also have denied, that the Letters produced at Westminster contained any clear or direct reference to the murder. She never denied that while the conspiracy was in progress she wrote letters to Bothwell, nor did she deny that she signed the Marriage Contract of the 6th April, which was declared to be in the handwriting of Huntley. This omission, and the omission also of Huntley to deny the genuineness of the Contract, are the more remarkable when it is remembered that she induced Huntley and Argyll to sign a statement implicating, so far as possible, the Earl of Moray in the plot against Darnley. Nor did the *asserted confession of Bothwell*, which formally declared that Mary was innocent of the Murder, contain any denial that such Letters were received by him from Mary. The Confession is supposed to have been *fabricated* by the friends of the Queen; but, whether fabricated or not, its *silence* in reference to the *Letters* is equally *significant*. When the Letters were published to the world in 1571 and 1572, Mary's silence regarding them, and the silence of her friends, remained practically unbroken. She had long had in her possession a version of the letters, and a copy of *Buchanan's Detectio* was sent her—undoubtedly with very bad taste—by Elizabeth. She bitterly, and perhaps with some justice, denounced in general terms the calumnious statements of the book, but *remained silent in regard to the letters*. Had they been founded on scraps of her own writing, had any of the letters been written by her to another than Bothwell, had they formed portions of a Diary, or been compiled from her stray and isolated memoranda, she would have detected this, and have thus supplied the CLUE *by which the forging might easily have been exposed.*

The apathy and caution of her friends, both in Scotland and on the Continent, in reference to the letters, is equally remarkable. The theory of forgery may have been hinted at, but it was never distinctly raised, nor was a proposal ever mooted by any of the great Catholic powers to have their genuineness tested. In like manner an ominous silence is maintained regarding them, not only in Mary's most confidential correspondence, but in the whole diplomatic correspondence of this period between the sovereigns of France and Spain and their ambassadors at foreign courts. To these sovereigns Mary appears to have made no direct appeal, or even any definite statement, in reference to the Letters; and, while they appear to have given no instructions to their ambassadors to make inquiries in regard to such a very vital matter, none of these ambassadors report any definite opinion regarding them.

If the Letters were forgeries, the Catholics come almost as badly out of the affair as the Protestants, if not even worse than they; for Mary, with all her faults, deserved at least to be condemned, if she was to be condemned at all, on true and sufficient evidence; and it is in any case clear that her enemies had stronger objections to her Catholicism than to her Murder of Darnley. On the supposition, however, that the Letters are genuine, the conduct of the Catholics needs no explanation or apology, and they come certainly better out of the affair than the Protestants. They, at least, as a party, were not in any degree responsible for the Murder of Darnley, but the same thing can scarcely be affirmed of the Protestants. It is impossible here to enter into a full consideration of the relation of the Earls of Moray and Morton, as well as other leading Protestant nobles, to the Murder of Darnley; but it may safely be affirmed that their passive attitude during the progress of the plot can hardly be attributed to entire ignorance that it was in progress; and that their conduct can only be excused from a consideration of the difficulty and peril of their position after Mary's escape from Holyrood. They out-manœuvred Bothwell and Mary, and either suffered, or *indirectly enticed them to commit the crime which occasioned their perdition*. All that can be plead for them is, that they were not in a position to control the conduct of Mary or Bothwell, or to be held responsible for the misdeeds on which both were bent. Nor could they deem themselves called upon to endanger their own lives by seeking to preserve the worthless life of Darnley, whose betrayal of their former plans cost thêm so dear. ☞ If Mary wrote the Casket Letters to Bothwell, she had become hopelessly incorrigible; and it cannot be affirmed that Moray, knowing his sister as he did, was acting either before or after the murder from motives of mere self-interest. Moray's estrangement from his sister dates from her marriage to Darnley. *With that marriage* also began her long series of misfortunes. They were partly due to Darnley's hopeless baseness and perversity. At any rate, so far as Moray was concerned in them, they are traceable rather to the absence of his guiding hand in directing his sister's policy than to the success of his efforts to subvert her authority. As regards Elizabeth, the question of the genuineness of the letters necessarily greatly affects the judgment to be passed upon her treatment of the Queen of Scots. Elizabeth's position—whether she believed the letters to be genuine or not—was one of enormous perplexity. She was placed in a cruel dilemma. It was dangerous to be severe, and yet the temptation to use severity was peculiarly strong. Mary was perhaps the most deadly enemy she possessed. She had awakened Elizabeth's ill will, not merely by laying claim to the English throne, but by the fame of her remarkable personal [?] charms. As the only great Protestant sovereign in Europe, Elizabeth's position was specially perilous. Though

Elizabeth had known the letters to be forgeries, she might have been excused for declining to aid her rival or to set her free; but indelible infamy would attach to the promulgation of such a vile calumny against her if it were baseless. On the other hand, if they were genuine, or if Elizabeth believed them to be so, it is difficult to discover any fault of a heinous kind in her treatment of Mary. Elizabeth's conduct was, perhaps, not consistent with strict rules of law or of equity—superficially it was marked by a hesitation, uncertainty, and fickleness—but, nevertheless, *if the letters were genuine*, not only was it characterized by a regard to broad principles of justice, but by considerable long suffering towards her unhappy captive, and by some merciful consideration for her, if not as a woman, at least as a deposed fellow-sovereign.

This painting of the head of Bothwell was made by a Danish artist, Otto Bache, when the coffin (supposed to be that of the Earl) was first opened in the year 1858. A sketch of this was taken by R. W. Macbeth, from which the present [photograph] portrait was produced by W. Greenoak Patterson, 1 Argyle Street, Edinburgh.

THE TRUE STORY OF BOTHWELL'S END.

BOTHWELL: A True Statement of his Career, which can be authenticated in every particular by incontrovertible evidence, between 15th June, 1567, when he parted from his wife, Mary Stuart, until his death in Dragsholm Castle, Island of Zealand, Denmark, in 1575-8.

Falsehood, frauds and, worse, forgeries, which pursued Bothwell during his life, did not cease even when hew as beyond the assaults of his enemies. They have been accumulated with almost as infamous virulence upon his memory as they were unrelentingly smirched upon his character while an exile and a prisoner. Perhaps there never was a stronger exemplification than in his case of the truth of Hallam's celebrated remarks in regard to the untrustworthiness of history.

Among other observations he says: "There is in general room enough for scepticism as to the characters of men who are only known to us through their enemies. History is full of calumnies, and calumnies that can never be effaced." Again, there is nothing so unhappily the rule than that "there is nothing so weak and helpless as Truth. She goes to the front without shield or spear. A good healthy Lie, clad in complete armor, with sword and shield, does the business."

Notwithstanding all the efforts of individuals and governments, of learning and industry, a screen, as impenetrable as the "Veil of Isis," fell over the last years of "the great" "Scotland's proudest Earl." His principal advocate, PETRICK, says, "*Then suddenly*—referring to the Autumn of 1571—ALL is SILENT! a great gap of four years occurs:—for what reason?" There is a solution and a plausible one. For six years the Danish government "had been tormented by the demands of Queen Elizabeth [of England) and the [successive] Regents of Scotland for the deliverance of Bothwell into their hands." Worn out with communications, reclamations, and declamations, Frederic II. "allowed the report of Bothwell's death to be circulated, and so put an end to all the worry on the subject." This accounts for the doubts as to whether Bothwell died in 1575, according to Petrick, or in 1577 or 1578 according to Schiern and others.

Belted Earl and husband of a Queen, his corpse rests in an unknown grave in a foreign land. Bothwell, from the Fall of 1567 until his decease—whenever it occurred— was "a Prisoner of Hope" in the hands of Frederic II., King of Denmark. This monarch was a curious character. He was at once the

Protector of Bothwell and his Custodian—whether at the last a severe or a lenient jailor nothing is definitely known. Falsehoods on the subject have been propagated industriously, but nothing trustworthy. That Frederic allowed him for years, pocket money, respectful attendance, company, and correspondence, sufficient means to dress in accordance with his rank and enjoy good cheer, is *certain*. In November, 1567, the King styles Bothwell "our particular Favorite" (Schiern, 332). In January, 1568, Bothwell was still living in Copenhagen, without anxieties for the future. When transferred to Malmo, it was

Malmo Huus.

still a sort of honorable confinement. His apartment was stately for the time. Even after this, down to 1571, velvet and silk were furnished for his attire, and his residence in Malmo, except as to duress, was anything but derogatory. He was purely a Prisoner of State and held in consideration. It was not until the 16th of June, 1573, that he was transferred to Dragsholm. Even then it is very doubtful if his confinement was as strict as represented. It is questionable if his treatment in Zealand was more rigorous or galling than that of Mary in England.

Bothwell was certainly better off in comfort and safety in Denmark than either one of his enemies, perishing in their prime and power by violent ends—deaths culminating in horror with the burning alive at the stake of the Scottish Lion King-at-Arms; sacrificed thus on his return to Scotland from his mission to Denmark to solicit the extradition of Bothwell, because, on the voyage home, he had learned too much of the villainy of Murray and his associates. A moral lesson is conveyed by a time-table presenting the miserable and often horrible manners in which those who persecuted Bothwell went to their last account. It is very comforting to his friends and admirers to learn this. Extracts from Marryatt's "Jutland and the Danish Isles" [Vol. I., 408–19], will serve to present a mingling of fact and fable in regard to Bothwell's last imprisonment and sepulture, which is about as true as tradition generally is—that is to say there is a basis of fact, but the superstructure is almost entirely fable.

In permitting Bothwell to leave her at Carberry Hill—when the winning cards were still in her own hands and while retreat to inexpugnable Dunbar was by no means hopeless nor even uncertain (Wiesener, 408)—with reinforcements coming up, which would have assured a victory to Mary, this determination

Hermitage Castle.

of the Queen to separate her fortunes from her husband has always, and in some degree justly, been brought forward, as to argument, that she had ceased to love him. Here once more Mary's principal biographer and advocate can be cited against herself and client, admitting (Agnes Strickland, II. 83–'4) that the Queen could be "ungrateful and unreasonable," subject to "strange infatuations;" "had taken her resolution"—devoid of

common sense, and blind and deaf to the lessons of experience—
"before she asked advice." If she had only shown a small portion of the energy she displayed eight months before, when, in the rough autumn weather, through a difficult country, and dangerous population, she rode on horseback fifty miles thither from Jedburgh and back to visit her lover, previously wounded in her service, in Hermitage Castle—his headquarters as Warden of the Marches (see Article "Jedburgh Abbey," *Saturday Review*, 30th September, 1882, page 439), Carberry Hill would have been a decisive triumph, instead of a disastrous and disgraceful catastrophe. It was simply the effect of cause; the inevitable quantities uniting in the product: *Ate* and Fate! If the reader would study the most flattering stories of her friends in the light of reason, not of feeling, they would find enough therein to condemn their heroine and absolve Bothwell. Froude's (VII., 369) exposition of her character is masterly, and its correctness is established more and more by comparison and investigation. If this stood alone there would be difficulty in meeting it.

"*In the deeper and nobler emotions she had neither share nor sympathy.* Here lay the vital difference between the Queen of Scots and her great rival, and here was the secret of the difference of their fortunes. In intellectual gifts Mary Stuart was at least Elizabeth's equal; and Anne Boleyn's daughter, as she said herself, was "no angel." But Elizabeth could feel, like a man, an unselfish interest in a great cause; Mary Stuart was ever her own centre of hope, fear or interest. *She thought of nothing, cared for nothing, except as linked with the gratification of some ambition, some desire, some humor of her own,* and thus Elizabeth was able to overcome temptations before which Mary fell."
"Whatever policy," said Randolph of her, "is in all the chief and best practical heads in France, whatever craft, falsehood or deceit is in all the subtle brains of Scotland, is either fresh in this woman's memory or she can fette it with a wet finger." (Froude, VII., 369). She was deluded by Kirkaldy as she had often been before by Murray; but her first act, after she discovered the awful mistake she had made in disregarding her husband's counsels, was to write to him, and send him a purse or sum of gold. She again wrote to him from Lochleven; she refused to separate her fortunes from his; her thoughts dwelt constantly upon him; and the very night of her escape from Lochleven, "while the men were stretching their aching legs, Mary Stuart was writing letters." *To whom?* To her uncle, the Cardinal of Lorraine, in Paris, for assistance, and *to her lover and husband*, BOTHWELL. She sent the Laird of Ricarton, a kinsman of Bothwell, to raise the Hepburns, united to the "great

Earl" by family and feudal ties, and make a dash on Dunbar to secure a port for the arrival of himself and of succor from France, and, when that port of entry was secured, to go on to Bothwell and tell him that she was free. Bothwell himself wrote to Frederic II. that he was on his way to Scotland to raise men and money when he was "treacherously captured" in Carmo-Sund (Norway). Ricarton did "go on," and found Bothwell in his confinement at Malmo. Another account says, as soon as she breathed the air of freedom, she despatched a messenger to find Bothwell, wherever he might be, and announce the happy tidings of her release, and summon him to her side, whence he never should have been permitted, for her security and honor, to depart.

Finally, to demonstrate the fallacy if not the wickedness of all this misrepresentation of Mary's feelings for Bothwell, to screen and excuse the Queen, even as late as the Spring of 1571, when she was at Sheffield, she was in correspondence with him at Malmo, and had written herself to Frederic II., entreating him NOT to listen to the persuasion of the Scottish envoy, Buchanan, laboring with so much enmity and earnestness against her husband. The correspondence must have been patent, for Buchanan told Lord Cecil that if he took the trouble he might intercept some of her letters.

That Lord Boyd, in 1569, obtained Bothwell's consent to the dissolution of his marriage, to enable Mary to marry Norfolk, shows that the intercourse between the Earl of Bothwell and the Queen, by letter and messenger, was still permitted. The fact is Frederic's whole treatment of Bothwell was regulated by the probabilities of Mary's restoration to her throne. It was not until her case seemed desperate that Bothwell was finally immured, *if he ever was actually thrown into a dungeon, which is very questionable.*

What became of Bothwell after they parted, forever on earth, at Carberry Hill, Sunday, 15th June, 1567, is soon told. He returned unmolested to Dunbar and remained there for several weeks undisturbed, although he did not confine himself to the fortress, but cruised about in the Firth of Forth, even penetrating beyond Edinburgh to the neighborhood of Linlithgow, to hold a meeting with Lord Claude Hamilton.

Of his political projects at this time no record remains. Confiding the defence of Dunbar to his kinsman, Sir Patrick Whitlaw, he sailed thence, in the beginning of July, with two light vessels and steered northward to visit his brother-in-law Huntley, at Strathbogie Castle, about ten miles south by west of Banff. His intention was, doubtless, to raise forces in the north-east and renew the struggle. The Queen had many friends in that quarter; adherents who did join her after her escape from Lochleven next year, 1568, and fought for her at Langside. Thence he proceeded to Spynie Castle, just north of Elgin, the residence of his aged great-uncle, Patrick Hepburn, Bishop of Murray, by whom he was brought up. Here a project was entertained to murder Bothwell, and a proposition to this effect was made to the English ambassador, Sir Nicholas Throckmorton, at Edinburgh. Whether the offer was rejected from policy or morality is not clearly shown. Some difficulty occurred, and Bothwell is charged with having slain one of his illegitimate cousins, who, in conjunction with two Rokebys, English spies, incited by greed, were plotting against him. The latter even offered to kill the Bishop as well as the Earl. Throckmorton seems to have objected to such a summary proceeding, because no advantage could be derived from the crime in favor of England and Elizabeth.

Bothwell now determined to visit his Dukedom of the Orkneys and sailed for the chief town of the group, Kirkwall. The opinion of those who have investigated the matter with most attention is that Bothwell—after his failure to enlist the active co-operation of his brother-in-law, Huntley—intended to proceed to the Orkneys, gather what strength he could and then, by way of Sweden, proceed to France to arouse the sympathy of Charles IX.—who, personally, was very friendly to him, and had confidence in the Earl, based on his services as "Chamberlain" at one time, and as "Captain of the Royal Scottish Body-Guard" at another—and derive from France, not only "the sinews of war," money, but actual military assistance. Fate, however, traversed all Bothwell's bold projects, and, *at Kirkwall, he was received with the treachery he had always experienced from those he had benefitted.* His Castellan, Gilbert Balfour, brother of Sir James Balfour, who had betrayed him after his marriage, and delivered up Edinburgh Castle to the Rebels—both accomplices in the murder of Darnley—turned the cannons of the place upon his feudal lord and benefactor. In consequence of this, Bothwell remained only two days in the port of Kirkwall, and then sailed northward to the Shetlands. Here he met with better treatment. The Bailiff, Olaf Sinclair, was a kinsman of the Earl's (now Duke's) mother, Jane Sinclair. Olaf received him kindly, and the people furnished him with supplies—a gratuity that was afterwards made the excuse for an onerous tax. Meanwhile, 19th August, Kirkaldy of Grange, Murray of Tullibardine, and the Bishop of Orkney, the same time-serving priest who actually had recently married Mary to Bothwell, sailed from Dundee with four ships of war, the best in Scotland, which, in addition to the seamen, carried four hundred picked arquebusiers (musketeers) as marines. The three commanders had authority to bring Bothwell, if taken, to a summary trial, and execute him. On the 25th August, 1567, the four pursuing ships sailed into Bressay Sound, on the shore of which stands Lerwick, the principal town of the Shetland group. At this date Bothwell's squadron consisted of four small vessels, two of which he had brought from Dunbar, and two Hanseatic armed Pinks, "two-masted lesser war ships" which he had HIRED at Sunburgh Head. One of these was named the "Pelican." Unconscious of danger, Bothwell's ships lay at anchor and a large portion of their crews were on shore. Bothwell, himself, at the time, was a guest of the Bailiff, Olaf Sinclair. Those in command who had remained on board, cut their cables and put to sea, and made their way to Unst, the most northerly of the Shetlands. In his pursuit, Kirkaldy ran his flagship, the "Unicorn," on a rock, and it went down. Bothwell meanwhile made his way by land to the Yell Sound, and thence by water to Unst, where he rejoined his ships. Thence he sent back one vessel to pick up his men who had been left on shore. With the other three he was overtaken, in the last days of August, by Kirkaldy with his three remaining ships of war. A hard fight ensued, which lasted for many hours. In the course of it, the mainmast of Bothwell's best ship was carried away by a cannon shot, and the south-west wind swelling into a fierce gale put an end to the conflict by dispersing the combatants. The Earl was driven with his two vessels out into the North Atlantic and one was captured. Running south by east, before the quartering gale, Bothwell soon traversed the 250 miles of ocean which separate the Shetlands from Norway, and first made the Island of Carmoe, twenty miles northwest of Stavanger, and was piloted into the quiet waters of Carm or Carmoe Sound. The ship had scarcely cast anchor when the Dano-Norwegian ship of war "Bjornen," Captain Christern Aalborg, made its appearance. By this Aalborg Bothwell *was treacherously captured* and carried into the port of Bergen. *There his case was investigated* by a commission or jury composed of four and twenty principal men of the town, of which ☞ *the foreman was Dr. Jens Skelderup, Bishop of Bergen* (Gaedeke, 396). *By them he was fully* ACQUITTED *of the charge of* "PIRACY," *with which his enemies had and have so consistently and falsely branded him*. There is not the slightest basis for such a charge. This was about 2d September, 1567. After this, the Governor of Bergen Castle showed Bothwell great honor and gave him a magnificent banquet. The Earl always mentioned this Governor with favor, and styles him "that good lord Erik Rosenkrands." Nevertheless, however courteously treated, Bothwell was, in fact, a prisoner, and when Captain Aalborg sailed from Bergen, 30th September, for Copenhagen, he carried Bothwell and some of his people with him. In the author's "Vindication of Bothwell," he has furnished the dry details of the Earl's detention in Denmark, of which the following is the summary. The King, Frederic II., would not consent to the extradition of Bothwell at the urgent requests either of the usurping Scottish government or of Queen Elizabeth, nor would he let him go free. Comparing lesser things with greater, it was exactly the case of "The great Apostle" and the Roman Governor, and Felix, willing to show the Jews a pleasure, left Paul bound. Frederic II. and Bothwell never met, but corresponded; Bothwell in French, which he spoke and wrote fluently. In a letter dated 18th November, 1567, the King designated Bothwell as "Our particular Favorite," and the Earl is styled in the correspondence "the Scottish King." On receiving Bothwell's statement, Frederic allowed him to remain at Copenhagen, supplying him with apparel suitable to his rank and liberal entertainment. In January, 1568, when the pressure of the Scotch Regency became stronger, Bothwell was transferred to Malmo Castle—then in Denmark, now in Sweden—on the northern shore of the Sound, about opposite Copenhagen. As the greater part of this castle was subsequently destroyed by fire or "submerged in the stormy waves," there is no certainty as to what portion was assigned as an abode for "the most distinguished State prisoner of Frederic II. It is supposed that he was located in a spacious apartment previously assigned to the Governor—a large, oblong, vaulted hall, with windows to the south looking out upon the grand panorama of the Sound; remotely to the West on the Island of Hven, the residence of Tycho Brahe; nearer on the Island of Salthon, opposite, and Amager beyond; in fact the whole interesting and lively environs of the Danish capital not farther distant than from ten to twenty miles. Meanwhile the King took care that his food and clothes should be rich and ample.

"He was detained there [Malmo] as a state prisoner indeed, but *led a luxurious life*, and was treated far better [?] than he deserved, being allowed the liberty of shooting and other recreations, while the King of Denmark ordered and paid for velvet dresses and other costly array for his use." When those "Titans of fraud" and crime, the Scottish authorities, empowered Colonel (Obrist or Oberst) and Captain John Clark, a Scottish mercenary—nominally commanding, in 1564, 206 Scottish cavalry-soldiers in the service of Denmark—to demand the extradition of Bothwell,

Bothwell turned the tables upon Clark by showing that when the Danish government sent Clark over to Scotland, in 1567, to enlist troops for its service, this agent was induced to expend the money entrusted to him for that special purpose for the benefit of the "Bonded" Lords in rebellion against Queen Mary and Bothwell, and actually marshalled the soldiers mustered in to serve Frederic, to fight against the Queen at Carberry Hill. Clark was sent before a court-martial, and, in spite of the remonstrances of Elizabeth and Murray, was found guilty, consigned to the same castle, Dragsholm, that eventually received Bothwell within its dragon ward, and died there a prisoner before his intended victim.

After this affair of Clark (1568–70), Frederic II. relaxed the restraint on the Earl and he was allowed full liberty within the precincts of the castle; nay more, he "was allowed no small liberty in Malmo, "dressing in velvet and silk, and leading a tranquil and by no means an unhappy life. In fact, except that he was not free (Wiesener, 505), "his life was that of a brilliant lord;" an existence far happier, perhaps, and certainly more comfortable, than that of the majority of potentates at this era. At a later date, it is said, Captain Clark became reconciled with Bothwell in Dragsholm, and, together, they drowned their cares and ennui in wine. This kind of living killed Clark in July, 1575, and seriously injured the health of Bothwell.

June 16, 1573, the reason why does not appear, Bothwell was privately transferred to the Castle of Dragsholm, Dragon's Island, now Adelsborg. Dragsholm appears to be an isthmus(island?) between the arms of Seiro Bay and the La(o)mme Fiorde, one of the arms of the Ise-Fiorde on the northwest coast of Zealand, 58 miles west of Copenhagen, off the road between the seaport towns of Holbeck to the east and Kallundsborg to the west. Faareveile, where the body of Bothwell *is said* to have been deposited, is on or near by the shore of La(o)mme Fiorde. According to generally accepted accounts, without trustworthy foundation however, Bothwell was plunged into a dungeon. This is mere surmise. ☞ *Nothing is positively known.* Even Agnes Strickland is forced to admit that the popular tradition of Bothwell's madness is entirely without foundation, and when at Dragsholm he was treated much better than he deserved; perhaps not worse than Mary was by Elizabeth. Schiern has demonstrated with greater clearness the UTTER FALSITY *of the Confession attributed to Bothwell.* [Larousse in his Grand Dictionnaire Universel, 1867, article "Bothwell," styles this rather legend than history, and adds the authenticity of such a confession is far from being sufficiently established. This, considering the manifold falsehoods told of Bothwell, is a fair statement, and Chambers' "Book of Days," 1864 (L, 783-4), gives another quite honest account of Bothwell's captivity, and mentions his having had a library, in which was a finely bound work, not on any frivolous subject, but on Arithmetic and Geometry, printed in Paris in 1538]. In all the authentic papers known to have been written by him, he insists upon his innocence, and with equal force alleges the guilt of Murray and Morton, and their associates. Even at Dragsholm it is stated that Bothwell "nevertheless got permission to go hunting." It is supposed that Frederic transferred the Earl from Malmo to Dragsholm to relieve himself from the annoyances of the applications made by the successive Regents of Scotland and the Queen of England. In her endeavors to injure Bothwell with Frederic II. and *retaliate upon the Earl, in his distress, for his lifelong patriotic refusals of her invitations to imitate* Murray, Morton, Kirkaldy and others, and become her tool and spy, and like Murray, her "fawning spaniel," and a traitor to his country, she descended to the meanness of styling Darnley as "King," whereas she had hitherto refused him that title, both while living and when dead, styling him, in her correspondence, "the dead gentleman," "*le mort gentilhomme*" (Buckingham, I.,363-64). Now she invoked vengeance upon Bothwell as the cruel assassin of his relative and sovereign. And here it may be pertinent to observe, that Bothwell was of the noblest blue blood on all sides. He was as nearly related to Mary as he was to his divorced wife, Jane Huntley, since he was descended from Joanna, daughter of James I., King of Scotland, and also from Queen Joanna or Jane Beaufort, wife of James I., by her second husband, Sir James Stewart, "The Black Knight of Lorn." That Bothwell was in any degree related to Darnley is not shown.

When and where did Bothwell die? Many say in Malmo-huus. Sheer ignorance! Shiern says 14th April, 1578; Petrick in the beginning of November, 1575, at Dragsholm. Whether he died in 1575 or 1578 there is nothing positive known of the details of his life after 1571.

The whole story of the close of Bothwell's Career (1567-1575'8), as a rule, in histories and biographies, is an utter calumny and sheer falsehood, and the whole secret of the LIES is summed up by the enigmatic absolution accorded by Pope Pius III. to the murderers of Cardinal Beatoun: "REMITTIMUS IRREMISIBILE," (*we pardon the* DEED *which does not admit of pardon*). Bothwell's crime—such a DEED—was FAILURE. Alas! Yes! "The Vices and Virtues are written in a language," most truthfully observed Lord Lytton, "the world cannot construe; it reads them in a vile translation and the translators are

𝔉𝔞𝔦𝔩𝔲𝔯𝔢 𝔞𝔫𝔡 𝔖𝔲𝔠𝔠𝔢𝔰𝔰 !"

Reproduction of a very rare old print, to show the relative heights of Mary, Queen of Scots. and her husband, Darnley, himself an exceedingly tall man.

☞ **Preserve this Cover and bind it in with Monograph, since it presents information important to the understanding of the work itself and furnishes explanations, &c., of the Illustrations and Text.**

COVER, PAGE 1.—The Germans call this Mary Stuart Casket CHATOULLEN—SCHATULLE—(wie Schachtel von dem Spatlatein (*Italienischer*) SCATULA, SCATOLA), Cassette particuliere (du Roi, du Souverain). Prof. KARL SACH'S "*Worterbuch,*" Band II., Seite 1485, Spalte 2.

The reproduction, on page 40, is known as No. 7 of the Series of Photographs from Portraits of Mary, Queen of Scots, executed by Caldesi and Montecchi, from the collection exhibited by the Archæological Institute, June, 1857. Paul and Dominic Colnaghi & Co., London, 1858: is a "Full length *Portrait* of the *Queen of Scots* and Darnley, engraved by R. Elstracke, and of excessive rarity, three impressions only being known to exist; photographed from that in a volume of Proclamations, in the Bodleian Library, collected in the reign of Queen Elizabeth. Another impression is in the Imperial Private Cabinet of Engravings at Vienna." This picture is introduced to attest the relative heights of Mary Stuart and her husband, who was known for his tall figure as the "Long Laddie."

PAGE 2.—Mary, Queen of Scots, from the original by Paris Bordone, Court Painter to Francis I. and Francis II., Kings of France, the latter grandson of the former and first husband of Mary Stuart. (As to discordant portraiture of Mary, see LEADER, 352-3.)

PAGE 3.—Portrait of Mary, Queen of Scots, is from the original in the Imperial Hermitage Palace, photographed and published with the authorization of H. M., the Emperor, by Charles Rœttger. A copy of this photograph was obtained by the writer through Hon. Wm. H. Hunt, United States Minister at the Court of St. Petersburg, in 1884. It is said that this picture was originally in the National or Royal Library, in Paris, was stolen therefrom during the first great French Revolution, and was sold in that city to a member of the Russian Legation, from whom it was purchased for the Imperial Gallery and assigned to the Hermitage Collection.

PAGE 4.—From a scarce print, done at the time (?), in the collection of J. Dent, Esq., M. P.

PAGE 6.—It is but honest to premise that no authentic portrait or likeness exists of James Hepburn, Earl of Bothwell, third husband of Mary Stuart; nor of Maitland of Lethington; nor of Kirkaldy of Grange. The likeness of Bothwell, on page 29, is photo-engraved from a photograph sent out to the writer by Mr. George Stronach, of the Advocates' Library, Edinburgh, Scotland. It bears the following legend: "A painting of the Head of Bothwell was made by a Danish artist, Otto Bache, when the coffin [containing the supposed remains of Bothwell] was first opened in the year 1858, a sketch of which was taken by R. W. Macbeth, from which the present [photograph] portrait was produced by W. Greenoak Patterson, 1 Argyle Sq., Edinburgh." The likeness of Bothwell, on page 6, is from an original characteristic sketch or drawing by the talented artist, J. O'B. Inman, son of Henry Inman, and one of the most famous painters of portraits in the United States. The original was prepared for "Bothwell: an Historical Drama." By General de Peyster; published in 1884.

PAGE 8.—The allusion to Lucretia Borgia in the verses is not made to the utterly depraved Lucretia of proverbial character, but the one whose offences are condoned by Gregorovius and other chroniclers, who represent her as the facile innocent victim of circumstances and of the ambition of her father and her brothers, accepting, without fuss or fury, husband after husband, as soon as each in turn was despatched, yielding herself the docile instrument of designing and unbridled Machiavelian statecraft. Between such a Mary as that, and the Mary of those who hold her responsible for all the evils done, is the only choice.

PAGE 12, Note.—"Objections to letters of Mary, Queen of Scots [to Bothwell], answered" [and answered with clearest argument against Mary]. Gentlemen's Magazine, 1796; vol. 66, 2d; pages 475-478; signature Peed. Divested of passion, Mary's "SCANDAL LETTER" to Elizabeth exhibits, according to LEADER, 559, "*a coarseness of language and of manners* that was *repulsive*, mingled with *an affectation of refinement* clothed in hyperbolic complement, making *pretence* to romance and chivalry, but *concealing the putrefaction of utter immorality.*" Mary's letters to NORFOLK likewise display the same unbounded submissiveness of will as the Casket Letters manifest subordination to Bothwell's wishes. (Consult Leader, 62, 63, 80, 111, 119, 120, 122, 246, &c.

PAGE 16.—The picture covering this whole page is reproduced from an old engraving, entitled "*Marie Stuart, Reyne d'Esscosse souffre le Martyre pour la Foy; et par la constance de sa mort, renouuelle en ces derniers temps, les examples* de l'ancienne Eglise." AUGUSTUS THUANUS; *lib.* 86. VIGNON *inuent.* MARIETTE *excud. cum priuil. Regis.* " From Figures de Vignon," vol. — —

PAGE 16.—Full length figure and likeness of Mary, Queen of Scots, is reproduced from the original engraving, in an old folio. The face of Mary in this picture closely resembles that of her mother, Mary of Guise, as engraved from the original painting by Jameson, at Leith. This figure likewise approximates closely to that in the portrait, *known to be authentic*, of Mary Stuart, now preserved in Hardwick Hall, one of the mansions of the Duke of Devonshire, of which a photograph was for the first time presented to the public in 1880.

PAGE 19, Note A.—"Deposition of Lord Home and Kirkaldy of Grange, regarding the cause of their defection from the party of James VI. [only acknowledged son and child of Mary Stuart], 31st July, 1593." "Appendix B." See T. F. Henderson's "The Casket Letters and Mary Stuart," pages 117-120.

PAGE 20, Note B.—Note "Kirkaldy," J.W. de P.'s "Bothwell: an Historical Drama." Kirkaldy was little or no better than the rest of the gang of "Bonded" Lords, although he exhibited some specious qualities, calculated to take with popular prejudice or opinion, always, as a rule, in error as to the intrinsic virtues of its favorites; witness instances of Pompey and Cæsar and a thousand other rivals:—the worst, but most plausible or jesuitical, always chosen as idols.

PAGE 22, Note C.—"The Impeachment of Mary Stuart," page 209.

PAGE 22, Note D.—John Skelton's "Maitland of Lethington and the Scotland of Mary Stuart." Wm. Blackwood & Sons, Edinburgh and London, 1887. DE PEYSTER'S MARY STUART COLLECTION, Columbia College Library.

PAGE 24, Note E.—Goodhall I., 41.

PAGE 29.—This portrait of James Hepburn, Earl of Bothwell, is from an original photograph sent out by Mr. George Stronach, of the "Advocates' Library," Edinburgh, Scotland, and was taken from a sketch by R. W. Macbeth, after a painting of the head of Bothwell by a Danish artist, Otto Bache, made when the coffin—simply supposed to be that of Bothwell—in the parish church of Faarveile (near the Castle of Dragsholm, in the island of Zealand, where Bothwell is reported to have died), was first opened in 1858.

Dragsholm Castle, where Bothwell was finally confined and died.

Printed by Libri Plureos GmbH in Hamburg,
Germany